Deadly Diseases

by Robin Twiddy

Minneapolis, Minnesota

Credits

All images courtesy of Shutterstock.com. With thanks to Getty Images, Thinkstock Photo, and iStockphoto. Cover and throughout – majcot, Vladimir Zotov, Olkita, Ramona Kaulitzki, Uglegorets, Cris Foto. p4–5 – conrado, Krakenimages.com, MATHILDE.LR, Ysbrand Cosijn, KrystianWozniak. p6–7 – Pixel-Sho, Rama, CC BY-SA 3.0 FR <https://creativecommons.org/licenses/by-sa/3.0/fr/deed.en>, via Wikimedia Commons, frank60, Martin Haas. p8–9 – pedalis, LoulouVonGlup, Oleksandr Kovalov1. p10–11 – Andrey_Kuzmin, Andreas Vogel, wavebreakmedia, Kateryna Kon, F16-ISO100. p12–13 – Rita Greer, FAL, via Wikimedia Commons, anatolypareev, Cosmin Manci. p14–15 – illustrissima, Nattika, Luis Echeverri Urrea, Andrii Symonenko. p16–17 – New Africa, Kaiskynet Studio, Armed Forces Institute of Pathology/National Museum of Health and Medicine, distributed via the Associated Press, Public domain, via Wikimedia Commons, Juan Gaertner, Rensselaer County Tuberculosis Association, Troy, N.Y., Public domain, via Wikimedia Commons. p18–19 – Everett Collection, ssuaphotos, Mariyana M. p20–21 – Kateryna Kon, Everett Collection. p22–23 – Margaret Suckley, Public domain, via Wikimedia Commons, Bernard Chantal.

Bearport Publishing Company Product Development Team

President: Jen Jenson; Director of Product Development: Spencer Brinker; Managing Editor: Allison Juda; Associate Editor: Naomi Reich; Senior Designer: Colin O'Dea; Associate Designer: Elena Klinkner; Associate Designer: Kayla Eggert; Product Development Specialist: Anita Stasson

Library of Congress Cataloging-in-Publication Data

Names: Twiddy, Robin, author.
Title: Deadly diseases / by Robin Twiddy.
Description: Minneapolis, Minnesota : Bearport Publishing Company, [2024] |
  Series: Can you believe it? | Includes index.
Identifiers: LCCN 2023001959 (print) | LCCN 2023001960 (ebook) | ISBN
  9798888220092 (library binding) | ISBN 9798888221952 (paperback) | ISBN
  9798888223246 (ebook)
Subjects: LCSH: Communicable diseases--Juvenile literature. | Diseases and
  history--Juvenile literature.
Classification: LCC RC113 .T85 2024 (print) | LCC RC113 (ebook) | DDC
  616.9--dc23/eng/20230131
LC record available at https://lccn.loc.gov/2023001959
LC ebook record available at https://lccn.loc.gov/2023001960

© 2024 Booklife Publishing
This edition is published by arrangement with Booklife Publishing.

North American adaptations © 2024 Bearport Publishing Company. All rights reserved. No part of this publication may be reproduced in whole or in part, stored in any retrieval system, or transmitted in any form or by any means, electronic, mechanical, photocopying, recording, or otherwise, without written permission from the publisher.

For more information, write to Bearport Publishing, 5357 Penn Avenue South, Minneapolis, MN 55419.

Contents

Outdated Ideas 4

Curious Cures 6

Leprosy 8

Black Death 12

Great Influenza Pandemic 16

Polio 20

Glossary 24

Index 24

Outdated Ideas

Deadly **diseases** have been killing people for thousands of years.

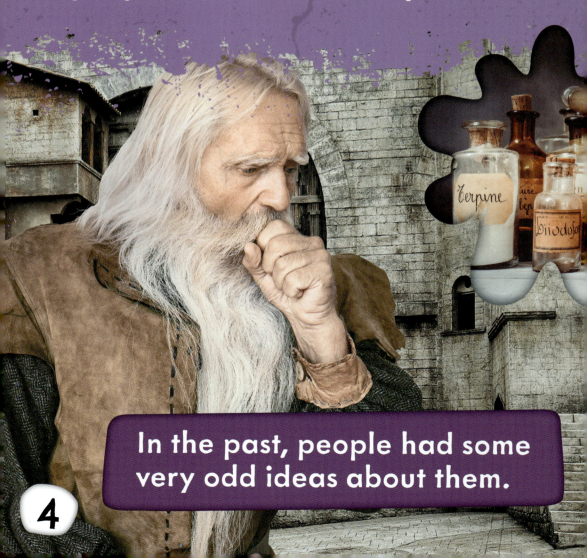

In the past, people had some very odd ideas about them.

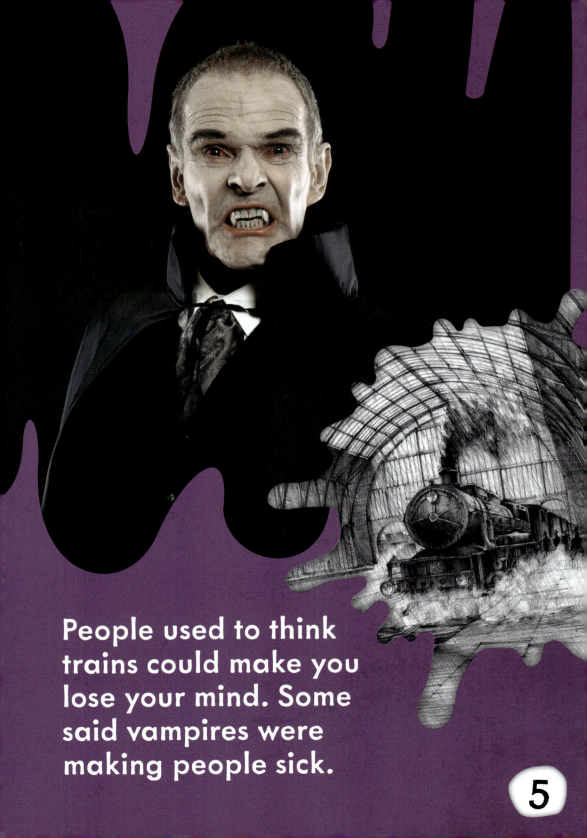

People used to think trains could make you lose your mind. Some said vampires were making people sick.

5

Curious Cures

There were some wacky **cures**, too.

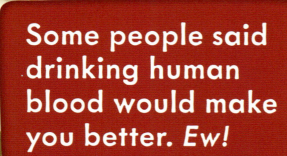

Some people said drinking human blood would make you better. *Ew!*

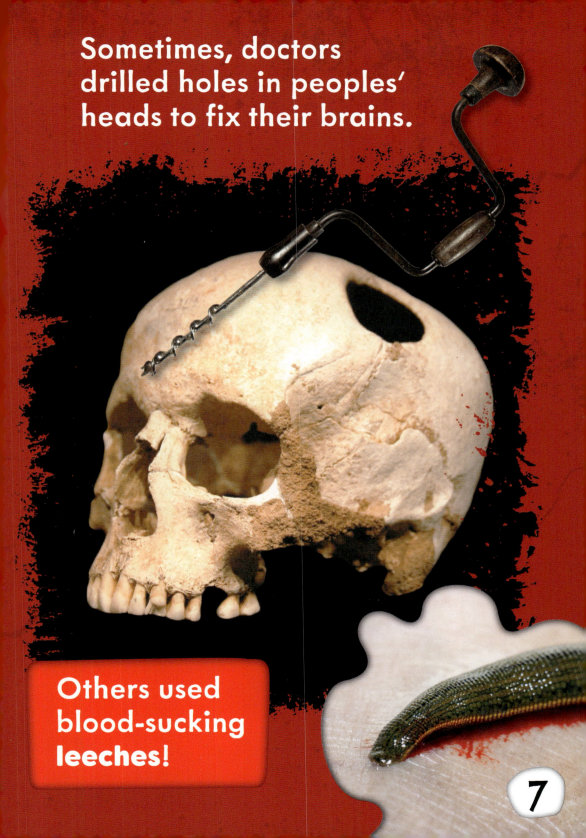

Sometimes, doctors drilled holes in peoples' heads to fix their brains.

Others used blood-sucking **leeches!**

Leprosy

Leprosy is a disease that harms your skin. It can make it hard to feel when you get hurt.

8

Some people used to think leprosy made you lose fingers.

However, this only happened if people hurt their fingers and did not do anything about it.

In the past, people with leprosy were sent away.

This stopped the disease from spreading.

Today, leprosy is called Hansen's disease. People can take **medicine** and get better from it.

This is leprosy close up.

Black Death

The Black Death was a disease that spread across Europe hundreds of years ago.

It killed about 25 million people.

The Black Death was probably spread by fleas living on rats.

Flea bites could give people the sickness.

Doctors who helped people with Black Death wore beak-shaped masks.

They kept dried flowers inside their masks to hide bad smells.

14

No one knew how to cure the disease. Some people tried rubbing onions on their skin! But, of course, that did not help.

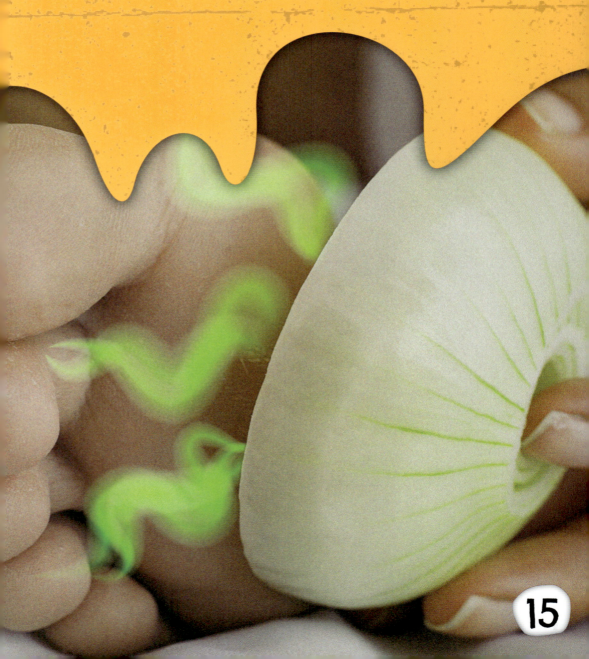

Great Influenza Pandemic

From 1918 to 1919, more than 50 million people died from a flu **pandemic.**

There were many things people tried to do to stay safe.

They covered their mouths and stopped shaking hands.

Still, this flu spread easily. Soldiers at war gave the disease to others as they traveled.

Some soldiers wore masks to stop the spread.

But mostly, soldiers tried to keep the flu a secret. They did not want the other side to think they were weak.

Polio

Polio is a disease that can stop you from being able to feel or move part of your body.

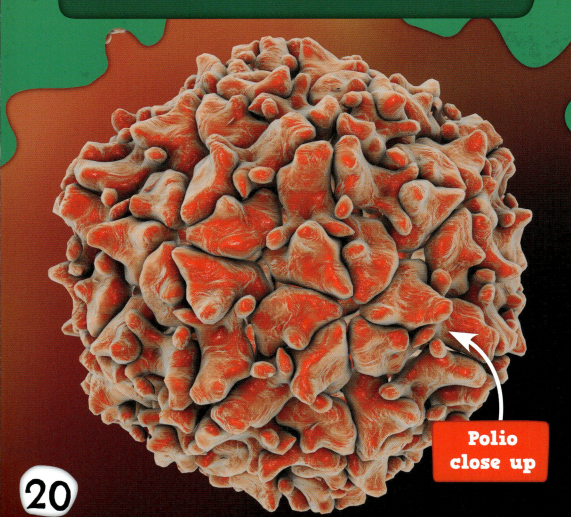

Polio close up

20

Some people with polio needed help breathing. They had to use a **machine** called an iron lung to stay alive.

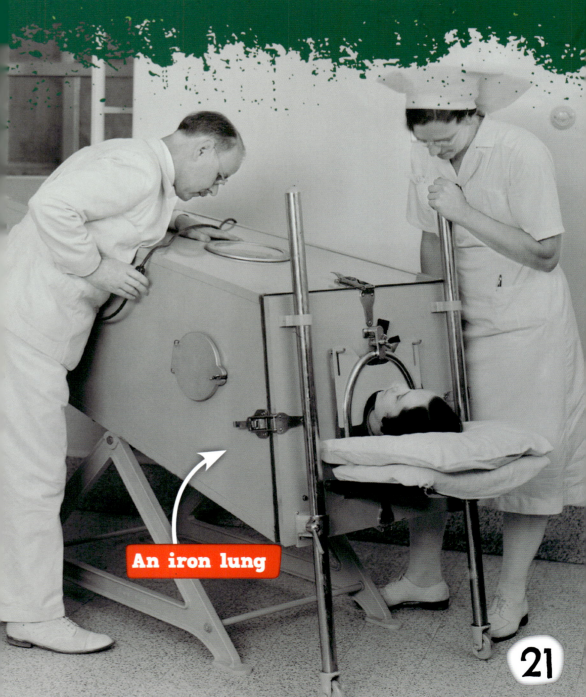

An iron lung

President Franklin D. Roosevelt had polio.

He helped raise money to make the first polio **vaccine**.

22

There is no cure for polio. However, vaccines have helped stop people from getting it.

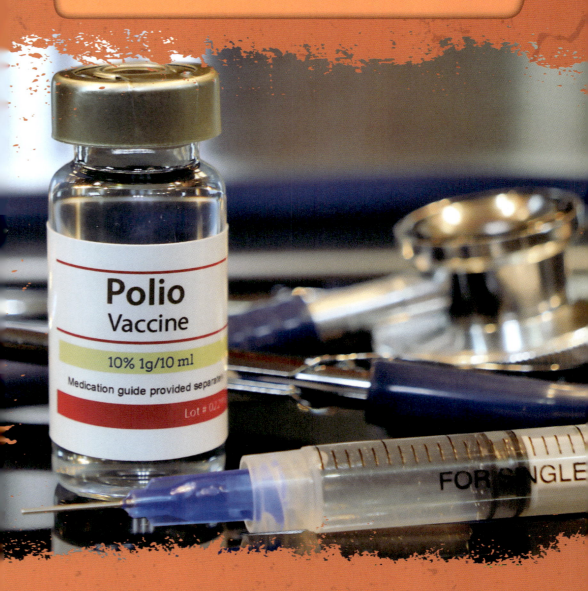

Today, polio is almost gone.

Glossary

cures things that can be done to heal or treat people who are sick

diseases illnesses or sicknesses

leeches worms with teeth that suck blood

machine a thing with moving parts that does work

medicine something used or taken to figh off sicknesses or pain

pandemic an outbreak of a disease that occurs over a large area and affects a lot of people

vaccine medicine that protects people against disease

Index

blood 6–7
brains 7
cures 6, 15, 23
fleas 13

flowers 14
iron lung 21
masks 14, 18
spread 10, 12–13, 18